INSIDE BRISTOL

Twenty Years of Doors Open Day

Bristol Doors Open Day, which goes from strength to strength, has been a great eye-opener for me and thousands of Bristol citizens. Penny Mellor deserves a huge thanks for having arranged the opening of such a remarkable variety of buildings of all ages and types over the past 20 years, and having documented it in this fascinating book.

It is a record of which Bristol should be extremely proud, long may the tradition continue.

George Ferguson CBE
Mayor of Bristol

INSIDE BRISTOL

Twenty Years of Doors Open Day

PENNY MELLOR

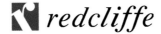 redcliffe

First published in 2013 by Redcliffe Press Ltd.,
81G Pembroke Road, Bristol BS8 3EA
www.redcliffepress.co.uk
info@redcliffepress.co.uk

The publishers wish to add their thanks to those organisations and individuals
listed in the author's acknowledgements for their generous support.

ISBN 978-1-908326-42-3
British Library Cataloguing-in-Publication Data
A catalogue record for this book is available from the British Library.

Designed by Stephen Morris, smc@freeuk.com
Printed by Short Run Press, Exeter

CONTENTS

DOORS OPEN DAY
1994

Saturday, 10th September

10.00am - 4.00pm

FREE ADMISSION

An open invitation to see some of Bristol's finest buildings

DOORS OPEN DAY *1995*

Saturday, 16th September

10.00am - 4.00pm

Open sesame and welcome into Bristol's history and heritage.

DOORS OPEN DAY 96

SEPTEMBER 14th

FREE ADMISSION
10AM - 4PM

An invitation to investigate Bristol's fascinating heritage

An invitation to investigate Bristol's fascinating heritage

DOORS OPEN DAY '97

13th September
10am until 4pm

DOORS OPEN DAY '98

12th September
10am until 4pm

FREE ADMISSION

BRISTOL DOORS OPEN DAY 1999

11th September
10am until 4pm

FREE ADMISSION

BRISTOL DOORS OPEN DAY 2000

16 September 10am - 4pm

FREE ADMISSION

BRISTOL DOORS OPEN DAY 2001

8 September 10am – 4pm

FREE ADMISSION

BRISTOL DOORS OPEN DAY 2002

14 September 10am – 4pm

FREE ADMISSION

BRISTOL DOORS OPEN DAY 2003

Saturday 13 September
10am – 4pm

NOW IN ITS TENTH YEAR
FREE ADMISSION

BRISTOL DOORS OPEN DAY 2004

Saturday 11 September
10am – 4pm

Free Admission

BRISTOL DOORS OPEN DAY 2005

Saturday 10 September
10am – 4pm

Free Admission

BRISTOL DOORS OPEN DAY 2006

Saturday 9 September
10am – 4pm

Free Admission

BRISTOL DOORS OPEN DAY 2007

Saturday 8 September
10am – 4pm

Free Admission

BRISTOL DOORS OPEN DAY 2008

Saturday 13 September
10am – 4pm

Free Admission

BRISTOL DOORS OPEN DAY 2009

Saturday 12 September
10am – 4pm

Free Admission

BRISTOL DOORS OPEN DAY 2010

Saturday 11 September
10am – 4pm

Free Admission

BRISTOL DOORS OPEN DAY 2011

Saturday 10th September
10am – 4pm

Free Admission

BRISTOL DOORS OPEN DAY 2012

Saturday 8th September
10am – 4pm

Free Admission

BRISTOL DOORS OPEN DAY 2013

Saturday September 14th
10am – 4pm

Free Admission

ACKNOWLEDGEMENTS

My grateful thanks to the many people who have contributed to this book. In particular:

Bristol City Council, Business West – The Initiative, and the Society of Merchant Venturers; John Savage and Simon Cooper (both members of the original Build a Better Bristol board); all of whom who have provided essential sponsorship without which this book could not have happened;

Gerry Brooke of the *Bristol Times*, to the spokespersons of the selected venues, and to the anonymous people who provided quotes;

Frances Gard who took the majority of the photographs – part specially commissioned, part from her work for Bristol Opening Doors, the Bristol Architecture Centre's Heritage Lottery 'Your Heritage' funded project; other photographs have been provided by the venues, those taken on the Day itself were mainly retrieved from the *Bristol Evening Post* archives by Simon Galloway and others are by my husband;

my husband whose support throughout the project has been much appreciated.

INTRODUCTION

September 2013 will be the twentieth year of Bristol Doors Open Day, the event when for one day each September places of historic and contemporary significance, not usually accessible or fully accessible, open their doors for free to the general public.

The idea of a Bristol open doors was first mooted at a meeting of the Building a Better Bristol sub-committee of the Bristol Initiative – a group of business and public sector workers dedicated to working together in the long-term interests of the city. One of the members, Tessa Jackson, then Director of the Arnolfini, had in 1990 been involved with a similar very successful opening of significant venues in Glasgow as part of their European Capital of Culture activities. (Hence the difference in name from the rest of England – Doors Open, the Scottish version – rather than Open Doors.) At the same time, as a result of a Council of Europe initiative, the UK Civic Trust was organising a national 'Open Doors' scheme with local civic societies, as were 26 other European countries.

That first year, 1994, Bristol Doors Open Day 'opened' twenty-eight buildings – the largest number of buildings open outside London – and there was much nervousness that no-one would come. In the event Bristolians turned out in their thousands on the day – and several of the venues were almost overwhelmed. The *Bristol Evening Post* which was celebrating its last year of using old-style printing presses, reported they had up to 4,000 visitors and had to resort to recruiting most of their staff, including their unsuspecting tea-ladies, into helping guide parties round.

Twenty years later some sixty plus venues participate each year – the total of venues is kept to about 60 for mainly logistical reasons – and over those intervening years more than 180 different Bristol venues have opened their doors. Some of those original venues, such as the Cathedral, or St. Mary Redcliffe, have been in each year since 1994; other venues are in for shorter periods depending on their own circum-

stances – opening is quite a commitment – or their numbers; and each year, so far, we have always found several interesting new venues to add to the list. Those not usually open to the public can, if they choose, just 'open their doors', those that are normally open have to lay on extra activities or provide access to otherwise unavailable spaces.

Over the years, people have had the opportunity to see inside an eclectic mix of Bristol buildings: from the third-century ruins of a Roman villa, to the twenty-first-century Bristol University's Centre for Nanoscience and Quantum Information; from the Mansion House, the Lord Mayor's grand residence, to the St. Julian's Nightshelter for Bristol's rough sleepers; from the uplifting Bristol Cathedral to the more mundane, but also fascinating, Bristol Sewage Treatment works.

The popularity of the Day continues to grow with over 50,000 visits recorded in 2012. Blaise House Museum wrote that for them 2012 had been 'the busiest we can ever remember for Doors Open Day'; Bristol Blue Glass SW that 'visitors had even come down from Manchester to participate and take the opportunity of exploring Bristol'; and Horizon House, home of the Environment Agency, had an unprecedented second-year three percent increase in visitor numbers over the previous year when they were in for the first time. First-time venues always have a high number of visitors, but second-year figures are usually significantly down.

How many 'visitors' are represented by that total of 50,000+ 'visits' can only be guessed at. If asked, I usually say that people probably average some four buildings at most (though most will not be as systematic as the couple I met in the Centre one year, who told me how they had been visiting four or five venues each year and had now – showing me the carefully ticked off list – seen all the venues on one side of the leaflet!). However on the other hand the *Bristol Evening Post* did once quote someone saying she had visited fifteen venues on the Day, and a mother of six wrote that they had gone round Redcliffe Caves three times, presumably counting as twenty-one visits in that year's tally!

Perhaps what gives me most pleasure is Doors Open Day's universal appeal to Bristolians. Some years back I was pressurised into doing a postcode survey of visitors. We had only a small number of responses from the thousands who went round – people don't go round Doors Open Day to fill in questionnaires – but from that small number I found I had every single postcode in Bristol well represented, as well as a host of others from further afield. In 2011 I did a similar exercise on the even smaller sample of the 500 or so who pre-booked into Aardman and Cameron Balloons and found a similar profile.

While our prime mission in Doors Open Day is to encourage Bristol residents to learn more about the city they live in, we also see our role as promoting Bristol to the outside world and it is pleasing to see the number of national companies that have mentioned it in their publicity statements. One year for instance I recorded that: EasyJet gave Doors Open Day as a reason for visiting Bristol in its inflight magazine; Lonely Planet mentioned it in their weekly mail out of 'Inspirational Things to Do in the UK this Week'; and the *Guardian* in its 'Things to Do This Saturday' column, with a record 3,717 venues opening in the national Heritage Open Days that weekend, chose to mention only Bristol ones. (Though for some reason they wrote: '...and see if Casualty, which is filmed in the city, is in any way realistic at the Queen Elizabeth's hospital...'. The head teacher at Queen Elizabeth's Hospital (QEH) school reported record numbers – presumably including some rather puzzled people...) The *Guardian* had also mentioned DOD and the Bristol University Centre for Nanoscience in an earlier leader – two days later the Centre had to withdraw because the building was not going to be ready on the Day.

The Day also appeals to all ages. One year I talked with one elderly lady, waiting at the bus stop for the Special Bus to The Roman Villa, who told me she had wanted to go to see it ever since it was first unearthed

in 1947 – whilst that same year the mother of an eighteen-month-old child wrote 'we nipped into St. Mary Redcliffe...and my toddler was fascinated by the tomb of a C15 knight – he thought it was someone sleeping'.

It has been difficult to select the thirty-one venues that are covered in detail here – after all, most venues in Doors Open Day have been on the list because they are 'significant' buildings. For the purposes of this book however I have looked to describe a range of venues that together illustrate the diversity of Bristol Doors Open Day. The text gives the history of each venue, and also highlights the hard work and very positive enthusiasm of all the owners and helpers who open their doors each year. It also shows the direct appreciation of a few of those thousands of people who go round on that second Saturday in September, having, as one wrote, 'a thoroughly good day out being a tourist in my own city'.

And so, my thanks to all the owners and helpers at Doors Open Day venues, to all our valued funders and supporters in kind over the twenty years and particularly to the Bristol Chamber of Commerce & Initiative and Bristol City Council; to the Tourist Information Centre at Harbourside team who nobly take bookings for venues that need it; to the *Bristol Post* for its splendid publicising of the event each year; to the members of my organising committee; and nationally to Heritage Open Days, the organisation that took over from the Civic Trust the national publicising of the event. Without all of these there would be no twenty years to celebrate and I am very grateful.

Penny Mellor,
Organiser Bristol Doors Open Day

Aardman Animation HQ   Gas Ferry Road

AARDMAN, THE BRISTOL-BASED world leader in model animation, produces feature films, television series and television commercials for both the domestic and international market. The studio has won four Oscars and been nominated for another six. Their output covers popular features such as *Wallace and Gromit*, *Sean the Sheep* and *Creature Comforts*, and the films *Chicken Run* and *The Pirates!* – to name but a few.

Work needing large-scale sets is filmed in sheds in Aztec West and Bedminster, but their headquarters and much of their creative thinking is based here.

The three-storey building, designed for them by Alec French Architects, provides office and studio space arranged around a tapered atrium providing breakout spaces, good daylight and air movement for the natural ventilation. The building is designed to be highly sustainable in both its materials and use of energy.

The main circulation is by way of galleries overlooking the atrium and placed outside the offices which are designed as a series of linked rooms. Breakout spaces and a laminated timber staircase, gently curved and free spanning between floors, also occupy the space.

There are many opportunities here for both informal dialogue and the exchange of ideas, and for Aardman's expression of their own very special character.

Tony Prescott, their Operations Manager writes:

'Aardman is committed to being in Bristol and we all love our dockside location so it was an easy decision to make to build on our existing central Bristol site. We now have room to wander around and be wonderfully creative!

'We are passionate about ensuring that all aspects of our business are environmentally sustainable. This is something that we struggled with in the past, working as we were in a motley collection of buildings and temporary structures that simply weren't sustainable for the business.

'Aardman has opened its doors for the big day in 2010 and 2011 and we are taking part again in 2013! On each occasion to date we have welcomed 300+ visitors to tour our HQ and experience the space that Aardman has enjoyed since moving in in 2009.

'Visitors on DOD seem to really enjoy the experience. The quality of the space combined with the cool stuff we have filled the building with (including four Oscars and a smattering of Baftas) results in highly positive reactions and a sense that people feel delighted to be here. We have had budding young animators bring their character creations with them and ask extremely technically challenging questions along with major fans of our characters hoping to catch a glimpse of one of our celebrities. Usually they aren't disappointed!

'There is a keen interest in the technical operation of the building and everyone loves the cinema...and the story that gets the biggest laugh...the feature staircase is held in place by Harley-Davidson bolts!'

ARNOS VALE CEMETERY Bath Road

ARNOS VALE CEMETERY, which opened in 1837, was one of many private urban cemeteries set up in cities and towns across the country to cope with overflowing city churchyards.

It was designed by the architect, Charles Underwood, in the style of a Greek necropolis. There are four fine buildings: a grand Corinthian-style mortuary chapel for the Anglicans, a simpler Ionic-style for the non-Conformists, and two Doric-style Entrance Lodges and offices – with the steep hillside behind terraced like an amphitheatre.

For many years Arnos Vale was the most fashionable place in Bristol to be buried. Among the more than 300,000 Bristolians buried there lies a complete cross section: Lord Mayors, industrialists, merchants, railway workers, social reformers…

By the end of the twentieth century, however, much of the cemetery was overgrown and neglected and in 1987 the owner of the site announced his intention to exhume the bodies and clear the graves to make way for housing development. There was outraged public outcry and a local pressure group was formed to try and secure the cemetery's safe future. It took another sixteen years – with much campaigning and failed negotiation with the owner, and over 20,000 people signing a petition to Bristol City Council to save it – before the City Council finally managed to purchase the site under a Compulsory Purchase Order.

Two years later a bid by the then well-established Arnos Vale Cemetery Trust to the Heritage Lottery was successful and the restoration of the cemetery buildings and 45-acre grounds could start, with Niall Phillips of restoration architects Purcell. Since then work has continued apace on the gardens, tombs and chapels, with each year newly restored places to visit. In 2012, for example, the Trust opened up the Anglican Chapel crypt for the first time enabling people to go beneath the chapel and see the vaults where their stonemasonry collection is stored, and the memorial plaques of the Bristol dignitaries interred there.

Arnos Vale first participated in DOD in 2004 after contact was made by the late Richard Smith, who together with his wife, Joyce – whose family are buried there – had been one of the founder members of the Association for the Preservation of Arnos Vale Cemetery. Despite much valiant work by Richard, Joyce and others, the cemetery was still in a largely overgrown state, graves at all angles from tree roots, and with many paths still completely inaccessible. That first year 600 intrigued visitors went round. And every year since there have been more newly restored buildings, graves and memorials to enjoy in this peaceful haven with its wildlife, many fine native trees, and magnificent exotic trees and shrubs surviving from the original Victorian plantings.

2004: The Evening Post reported in August that 'A £1Million fund raising campaign will be launched coinciding with Doors Open Day on September 11th'. The leaflet cover that year was a splendidly atmospheric photo of the site; and Richard and I sat amongst the graves being interviewed by the BBC on the Friday before the Day.

2005: Cemetery was awarded £4.8m in December by the Heritage Lottery Fund towards its restoration.

2006: In March Richard Smith wrote to me: 'we will definitely be able to open the West Lodge this year for DOD as we have just moved into it!'

2007: Work was completed in the spring of removing some of the self-seeded trees and other undergrowth generally, to form widened access corridors based on the original drives and footpaths.

2008: Major building restoration work finally started in March and after Doors Open Day that year they wrote 'Even though the cemetery was more building site than buildings we had 330 visitors and were very pleased!'

2009: The HLF funded work was completed in October.

Restoration work continues.

'A haven of tranquillity and breathtaking sights.'

'What a lovely oasis of calm it is, beautiful grounds, very interesting tombs & mausoleums – reminders of a long gone age.'

BRISTOL CATHEDRAL   College Green

BRISTOL'S CATHEDRAL began as an Augustinian monastery in the mid-twelfth century, expanding over the centuries and finally being completed in the nineteenth century.

Parts of that original Abbey remain. In particular, the almost unaltered Chapter House, dating from c.1150 AD, is a fine example of late-Norman architecture. There the monks, seated round the edge of the room, would gather after morning mass to discuss the business of the day.

In the main body of the Cathedral, the Elder Lady Chapel in the north transept dates from around 1220 AD. Around the walls at eye level the detail of the medieval carvers' images are worth seeking out. Faces of men and monkeys peep out from the intricate stone foliage, a fox carries a duck and a goat has a rabbit slung over its shoulder.

The Lady Chapel at the east end was completed about a century later and the central tower, more that 100 feet high, is fifteenth-century. The twin towers to the west however were not built until Victorian times.

Fragments of earlier stained glass can be found in various of the windows, but the stained-glass windows, immediately to the left as you enter, are of the twentieth century. These are a memorial to the uniformed members of the various organisations who served on the Home Front in the Second World War.

On the Day the Cathedral, as part of their 'special access,' have of recent years given very popular tours up the central bell tower, with visitors guided past the original solid oak bell frame, still with three of the original bells, and – weather permitting – out onto the roof.

In 2005 they also ran a Living History project on DOD commemorating 60 years since the end of the second World War. The child, Clive Odey, who featured in one of the Home Front stained glass windows showing a nurse comforting a young child, was to be present talking to visitors about his experience as a child in the Blitz. The Bristol Evening Post *in its lead-up to DOD publicised the fact, resulting in some unscheduled results:*

On the Day Mr. Odey, by then in his 60s, was duly reminiscing beneath the window to an appreciative audience – when he was joined, to his, the visitors' and the Cathedral's delight, by three of the nurses who had tended him in the war and who had read in the paper of his appearance.

I wrote of the event in the Report of the Day I send to all venues each year and heard back from Jill Milne, of St. Monica's – also a venue that year:
'One of our residents, Miss Ellis, was a nursing sister in the war and she is also depicted in the window of Bristol Cathedral. I understand she saved the lives of some children in the Children's Hospital during a bombing raid. She is shown holding the hand of the little boy.'

BRISTOL CENTRAL LIBRARY   Deanery Road

AT THE BEGINNING of the seventeenth century Bristol possessed the second earliest public municipal library in England thanks to bequests by two of its citizens – a fine book collection and a venue at the north end of King Street (today a Chinese restaurant).

By the end of the nineteenth century, however, with increasing demand in Victorian times for library services, the King Street building, although expanded in the mid-eighteenth century, had become seriously inadequate.

A new, spacious building was much needed but no money was forthcoming until a lover of the arts, the banker Vincent Stuckey Lean, left the Corporation £45,000 in his will. (His portrait can be seen on the stairs leading up to the Reference Library) £45,000 was a very substantial sum – equivalent to some millions today – more than enough to pay for a fine new building and one that befitted the city.

After considering King Street, and also a site where the Hippodrome stands today, the council decided to build next to the old Abbey Gatehouse, off College Green. In 1902 they held an architectural competition – won by a London firm, H. Percy Adams and designed by Charles Holden, then working there as an architectural assistant.

Holden carefully produced a building facing Deanery Road, fitting in with the medieval gatehouse next door, with the bulk of the six-floor building cleverly contained on Lower College Green and with elevations that were precursors of the Modern Movement in architecture.

Internally, the building has three showpieces – the entrance hall with its vaults and piers, the grand reference library and the historic Bristol Room designed around the fittings of the original first-floor reading room in the King Street library.

For DOD the Library lays on 'behind-the-scenes' tours – some 90 minutes long and inevitably with lots of stairs – but always really popular and well-received, says Kathy McDermott, the Stock and Reading Librarian:

'We start the tours outside the front of the Central Library, give some background about the history of libraries within Bristol – we are coming up to 400 years of libraries in the city. Lots of interesting historic 'facts' eg prostitutes checking Lloyds List newspapers to see which ships were due in port; miscreants being given six months' hard labour as punishment for stealing library books. We look at the exterior – front and back – before coming back inside to the foyer, when we talk about how the lay-out of the library has changed.

'Then upstairs to the Reference Library corridor, and into the Bristol Room with an overmantel by Grinling Gibbons, chair said to have been used by Judge Jefferies dealing out justice to the Monmouth rebels of 1685 during the Bloody Assize, and bookcases from the library in King Street.

'The rest of the tour is behind-the-scenes. We go up to the top of the building (where the library ghost has allegedly been seen – though not on a tour, unfortunately!) and get out some of the library's treasures, e.g. the Nuremburg Chronicle *from 1493, for people to look at.*

'Then we go down through the stacks where old volumes of newspapers, books and periodicals are kept and also talk about how books are delivered back and forth across the city and beyond.'

'What a day! Record numbers for the six tours we did around the Central Library – 165 people. We also had crib sheets for people who couldn't get onto the tours, so many more people also looked around without being 'led', as it were. We had great response from people, and the whole day was really incredibly positive.' (KMcD)

BRISTOL HEART INSTITUTE off Horfield Road

THE BRISTOL HEART INSTITUTE which opened in May 2009, is a new high-quality addition by CODA Architects to the Bristol Royal Infirmary. It provides for the first time in Bristol a full range of state-of-the-art diagnostic and interventional treatments for heart conditions under one roof. There are three catheter laboratories for cardiology diagnostic procedures and treatments, three operating theatres for open-heart surgery and one hybrid catheter laboratory / theatre, where surgeons and cardiologists carry out joint procedures. Cardiac services are currently delivered to some 10,000 people in Bristol and the South West each year.

Located behind the main hospital buildings on the Kingsdown slopes the building is a welcome contrast, both externally and internally, to the 1950s and 60s architecture of earlier buildings on the site. There was extensive consultation on the design of the interior with staff, patients, and visitors. For example, patients had noted that when they are being wheeled through the hospital on beds, the main thing they could see was fluorescent lights – so an artist was commissioned to decorate the patient lifts' ceilings (see opposite) and the walls of the lift-lobbies. For visitors and those waiting for appointments, the elegant top-lit atrium is calming, legible and well signed, and includes extensive artwork. Medically, to quote their Matron, it provides: 'twenty-first-century facilities in a twenty-first-century building.'

The BHI first approached us a year or so after they had settled in about their possible participation in Doors Open Day, and after a sample guided tour to see what they were offering, we welcomed them into DOD 2011. It was definitely a 'significant contemporary building'.

That year the BRI was in the midst of extensive building works on the Horfield Road site (as it still is in 2013), so just getting to the building wasn't easy. There was no need to worry though – that first year over 400 intrepid DOD visitors found their way!

Their Communications Manager, Fiona Reid, wrote of DOD 2012:
'We had guided tours to the laboratories and theatres leaving as soon as we had a group of visitors together – approximately every ten minutes.

'Obviously we couldn't go into the theatres, but we opened up one of the three catheter labs to see into and one of our specialist nurses did a great job of explaining what happens there and in the theatres.

'Talks were also given by our staff on various topics throughout the day in the atrium.

'We also had guided tours onto the roof of the building from where you can see all the building work and have a lovely view of Bristol.'

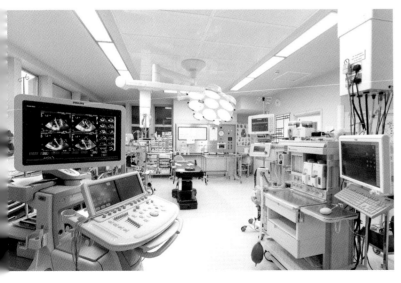

BRISTOL MUSEUM & ART GALLERY   Queen's Road

THE BRISTOL MUSEUM AND ART GALLERY have been in their Edwardian Baroque-style home since 1905 – or at least the Art Gallery, along with antiquities, has been. Until being blitzed in the Second World War the Museum with its great natural history and geological collections had been separate, housed next door in what is now Brown's restaurant.

The Art Gallery was established thanks to the generosity of the millionaire tobacco baron, Sir William Henry Wills. He was very keen that Bristol should have a municipal art gallery on the lines of those funded by wealthy businessmen in several northern cities and towns. His cousin Sir Frank Wills was the architect.

Today the museum houses a marvellously eclectic collection of natural history, archaeological and geological objects, glass, ceramics and china ware and a fine Egyptian department; whilst the art gallery has a selection of mainly British art, including work by Bristol School artists, that Sir William would surely be proud of.

One might wonder though what he would have made of their 2009 unconventional exhibition – the works of the Bristol graffiti artist, Banksy?

In an exhibition titled 'Banksy vs Bristol Museum', the artist integrated his works throughout the Museum and the Art Gallery. In the 12 weeks it was on it brought in more than 300,000 visitors from all over the UK and internationally – confirming Bristol's reputation as a vibrant city and injecting £15M into the local economy. And it was great fun.

The public galleries of the City Museum are a popular venue throughout the year and on top of that, some 1,500 visitors visit on Doors Open Day each year.

Most day-to-day visitors know nothing of the behind-the-scenes activities that go on there and so on the Day the Museum also 'opens its doors' to the building's curatorial activities, laying on tours to normally non-public spaces.

Ray Barnett, the Collections Manager (who was himself on that original Build a Better Bristol Committee) writes: 'Some eighty to ninety people can sign on to these tours – they last for an hour and a half and there are lots of stairs, but everybody seems to happily stay the course. Numbers on tours at the Museum & Art Gallery, are restricted by our own resources to deliver rather than by demand!

'People go through the basement stores of Archaeology, World Cultures, Natural History, Fine and Decorative Art and Geology, through the conservation labs (general artefacts, oil painting and works on paper), the technicians' carpentry workshops, design and learning team offices, schools room, admin and curatorial offices, past the painted windows of the front and finally back into the public galleries.'

'The tour was amazing and such an informative time and a great insight and friendly – the 90 minutes went in a flash.'

BRISTOL OLD VIC King Street

THE THEATRE COMPANY Bristol Old Vic has been based at the Theatre Royal in King Street since 1946.

The theatre contains Britain's oldest surviving theatre auditorium, designed in 1766 by Thomas Saunders and Thomas Paty. It expanded in the 1970s into the adjacent eighteenth-century Coopers' Hall, adapted and extended by architect Peter Moro. And recently, under Andrzej Blonski Architects, the theatre complex has undergone refurbishment that provided much needed improvements to the stage, theatre, auditorium, backstage and rehearsal spaces.

Whilst the theatre was closed, the company continued to present work in the Studio and Basement spaces, as well as at other sites around Bristol – notably *Treasure Island* in King Street itself. The Theatre Royal re-opened in autumn 2012.

From the 'Pit' (i.e. the ground-floor level of seating) to the gallery (the top floor), the sightlines have been dramatically improved and the theatre now boasts a new 'thrust' stage – not only placing the actors and audience closer together, but allowing the possibility of programming work (like concerts) with the front five rows removed and given over to standing room directly at the front of the stage.

There are also new rehearsal spaces, a new lift backstage to make the whole building accessible; improved air-flow, mechanics and insulation to make the building a safer, greener space and, most importantly, the seating has been replaced with state-of-the-art comfortable, custom-made seats.

Joe Spurgeon their Marketing Manager writes:

'Whenever productions and rehearsals permit, Bristol Old Vic has been a proud part of Doors Open Day.

'On the Day, you can see all of these things, making Bristol Old Vic one of the most popular stop-off points during the day. Small groups have a whistle-top tour of the theatre's many intriguing corners and curios.

'Visitors on the tours:

Start in the Pit and uncover the history of a theatre which is pregnant with stories from times gone-by, including Sarah Macready who single-handedly ran the theatre for several years during the 1800s and whose ghost still allegedly haunts the building.

'Walk the stage which has been graced by generations of world-famous actors including David Garrick, Sarah Siddons, Daniel Day-Lewis, Jeremy Irons, Patrick Stewart, Peter O'Toole and countless others.

'Unpack the sociology and pastimes of a generation where the theatre – a wild, heady, riotous place of entertainment – was the place to be seen and used to boast wooden spikes fixed to the front of the stage to keep the braying masses back. During the recent redevelopment, amongst century-old sweet wrappers, tickets and china, 200-year old orange peel and remnants of pigs' trotters – a nineteenth-century precursor to pork scratchings – were uncovered.

'And elsewhere, at the theatre's apex, steal a glance at the country's only surviving "thunder run"; a precision-engineered series of sloping wooden troughs that, with the addition of a rolling cannonball, was used to depict the sound of thunder overhead.'

BRISTOL PORT   Avonmouth and Royal Portbury Docks

UNTIL THE NINETEENTH CENTURY Bristol's busy port was entirely located in the city centre. However, as vessels increased in size and draught, navigating the river Avon into Bristol became increasingly difficult. In 1870, therefore, a new dock basin was established at the mouth of the River Avon at Avonmouth.

Throughout the twentieth-century Avonmouth developed as a port, but vessels were becoming even larger and again a new dock basin was needed to handle them. In 1978 Royal Portbury Dock opened on the opposite (southern) side of the River Avon.

In 1991 the port was privatised. Two entrepreneurs bought it from the City Council and over the ensuing years invested over £450m in technology, equipment, facilities and skills.

Since privatisation, annual tonnage through-put has increased from 4m tonnes to 12m tonnes and revenues from £22M to £75M. The Port is recognised as among the most productive and technically advanced in Europe. It is Britain's most centrally located deep sea port and, with excellent motorway access and good rail connections, it is able to access a population of 45 million people living within a 300km radius.

Bristol Port handles a massive range of products from coal and biomass to generate electricity, to animal feed, cars, metals, paper, and consumer food and goods.

Sue Turner, Director of Communications at the Bristol Port Company, writes: 'As an island nation 95% of UK imports come by sea, so ports are vital to all of us, but for obvious security and safety reasons the Port is normally out of bounds to the public. However in 2012 we were delighted to take part in Doors Open Day for the first time in order to give people a behind-the-scenes view of this important local business.'

No building doors to open here but instead, well secured and guarded gates, as Sue took four large coach loads of Doors Open Day visitors on hour-long tours into both the Avonmouth and Portbury docks areas.

The tours surveyed the old and newer parts of Avonmouth, including getting close to the landmark wind turbines. After traversing the M5 with a view of the car storage areas, visitors viewed the very modern facilities at Royal Portbury Dock including the largest locks in Western Europe, the animal feed sheds and one-million-tonne coal stockyard.

'My husband and friend joined your coach party at 13:00 today and some seven hours later they still haven't stopped talking about it yet. They came home full of information and admiration for the way it was imparted.'

'My early career in logistics was in the port. To be able to rekindle those moments, that I enjoyed so much, was really exciting…and what better way to see it than on such a professionally organised tour. I loved to be able to see the changes and the growth first hand. To see all the ships coming and going sent a shiver down my spine. But what I found most exciting was that the port was, positively, still meeting its challenges with its partner, the sea...'

'We live in Portishead and within sight of the docks, so like to identify individual ships and the cargo they are carrying. But we had no idea that the range of cargoes was so diverse or that there was such a range of other supporting businesses.'

BRISTOL RECORD OFFICE   Smeaton Road

THE RECORD OFFICE was established in 1924 to look after the official archives of the City of Bristol, and to collect and preserve many other records relating to the City and surrounding area. Initially sited in the Council House, it moved from there in 1992 to larger, and newly converted, premises in the western part of B Bond on Spike Island.

B Bond, designed in 1908 by W.W. Squire, the City Engineer, was originally a bonded warehouse serving Bristol Harbour – that is a secure building in which dutiable goods, in this case tobacco, could be stored until duty had been paid.

The 9-storey red-brick-clad building was designed in two equal parts, with originally open-plan floors separated by a central spine wall. The two parts of the building are now both used by the Council – the Bristol Record Office to the west and the Create Centre, set up by the council to promote environmental awareness, to the east.

Allie Dillon Senior Archivist (Public Services):
'Here at Bristol Record Office, we offer behind-the-scenes tours of our strong-rooms on Doors Open Day, starting by covering the history of the bonded tobacco warehouses and going on to show how B Bond is now used to preserve and store the city's archives. Throughout the tours, we show examples of records to demonstrate the wide range of material we hold, from medieval charters and letters patents (from c.1191 onwards) to modern examples from collections such as the Arnolfini archive. The tours are very popular – visitors are often surprised to discover that so much of the City's history survives on record and that we exist to make these documents available to the public.

'As the tours are always oversubscribed, we also screen archive footage of Bristol from our unique film collection. In addition, the Bristol & Avon Family History Society research room is open for their members to offer genealogy advice to visitors and where we always have an exhibition of local history interest on display. This year (2012) we held a dual exhibition with Clifton Rocks Railways over Doors Open Day.'

Maggie Shapland of Clifton Rocks Railway adds: 'It was of mutual benefit – it brought more visitors to the Record Office than a normal Doors Open Day and we at the Rocks Railway were able to show things we cannot normally display. Also Clifton Rocks Railway visitors had the complete experience of getting from one site to the other by time-appropriate means – first getting on a period bus and then on a steam train.'

[On Doors Open Day the Bristol Omnibus Vehicle Collection run free rides on a vintage Bristol Bus between the Rocks Railway and the At-Bristol car park; and the Harbour Railway steam trains run between M Shed and B Bond.]

'Absolutely fascinating, excellent event – could have spent days rather than hours here. Will definitely come again. Staff were very helpful, friendly and informative.'

BRISTOL SEWAGE TREATMENT WORKS Kingsweston Lane

THE SEWAGE WORKS at Avonmouth opened in the early 1960s. Until then over 25 million gallons (some 115 million litres) of sewage was being discharged each year into the Avon – with around 200 tonnes of chlorine added in an attempt to disinfect the flow.

Today, nearly twice that amount flows into the Avonmouth works from Bristol's four major sewage systems carrying the waste from more than a million people. In addition industrial waste from local businesses that have agreements with the works comes in tankers to be treated. And now biological processes and bacteria that occur naturally in rivers and lakes are used to clean the flow – the bacteria being provided with optimum conditions to feed and reproduce so as to dramatically speed up treatment.

The sewage works have been 'opening' for DOD on and off since 1995, getting between 300 and 400 people each year, many coming on the Special DOD bus to be shown round in small groups by Bob Porter and his team.

It is a fascinating ninety minutes tracing at close quarters the moment from when the raw sewage comes on site, to when the final clean effluent is pumped into the Severn estuary or the Seabank power station cooling system.

Visitors are led up, down and around an impressive array of pipes, tanks and machines performing these operations – all the while having the undergoing process clearly explained in simple terms.

They see the effluent being raised up with large Archimedes screws; non-biological waste, grit and other such foreign bodies being filtered out and taken away for composting; and the resultant 'sludge' being settled, 'anaerobically digested' – and turned into fertiliser.

The whole process takes some fourteen days from beginning to end. It is amazing to learn that such a complicated process ends with surplus power being fed back into the National Grid!

[Four large wind turbines are also currently planned to come on site in 2014 that will feed back even more.]

Bob Porter, manager of the Sewage Treatment Works, who started there as a fitter back in the 1980s, says:
'These days, with the sewage treated to such a high standard, it's hard to believe that [the pre-1960s treatment] was ever allowed. Now the water coming out at the end of the process is incredibly clean when we pump it into the Severn.

'It's amazing how much reusable material we're able to get out of all this waste, whether it's the electricity that's generated from the methane gas, the water for cooling the local power station, or the sludge that's transformed into a fertiliser. In fact, these days, there's very little waste at all – my goal is to have none!'

BRISTOL SOUTH SLIPPER BATHS Dean Lane

BRISTOL SOUTH BATHS were built by Bristol Corporation in 1931, one of several 'modern' baths built by the City in the 1930s for the 'health and hygiene of its citizens'.

Designed, according to its architect, C.F.W Dening, along lines 'reminiscent of the Later Renaissance Period' but in a manner 'sufficiently modern to proclaim the date of its erection and its function' – the Baths provided a main swimming pool hall with segregated slipper baths running in a separate room down the pool's west side.

The slipper baths proved exceedingly popular. Most of the houses in the area, built in the late nineteenth century for workers in the local coal mining and tobacco industries, would not at that time have had a bathroom, or often not even an internal water supply – and some 100,000 people (most on regular visits) passed through the turnstiles in the summer of 1931.

After the war, as houses began to have their own sanitary arrangements, the slipper baths became increasingly redundant and were finally closed to the public in the 1960s.

'Another bit of hidden Bristol. Great to see and imagine the luxury of a weekly bath! Particularly good to see the pride and detail expressed in the architecture.'

'It was like going to a museum. It was really cool and I liked the buttons.' Emma (8)

'Awesome :–)' Mena (13)

'Fantastic opportunity to revisit a piece of social history embodied in a building. This sort of bathing facility is so rare as a survival – please try to get the fabric repaired and preserved.'

Bristol South Baths was a very late entry into Doors Open Day 2012. I had been shown round back in April and had happily agreed that it would be a good candidate – providing the organisers had Council agreement and insurance. In fact it was only finally able to be advertised as participating just a few days beforehand. Thanks to modern methods of communications however we could put it on the DOD website, the South Pool Friends tweeted, face-paged and rang round – and they ended up showing some 100 people round.

[Chair, Friends of Bristol South Pool]: 'We had looked into the Men's 1st class Slipper Baths on a few occasions with a torch. They were dirty and all rubble from when they boarded over the skylight & covered the floor. We could see, though, that the baths were intact, noticed they were made of marble terrazzo and realised that they could be quite beautiful with a bit of a clean. The baths had been described by the council as dilapidated, but this really was not the case at all, which was quite exciting!

'After negotiation with the council they agreed to allow one of the Baths to be cleaned up. A contractor cleared out the rubble, made it safe, and rigged up lighting. Then the Friends of the Pool came in, gave everything a really good scrub, and popped some props in.

'Everything was all a bit last minute, and we advertised it as a venue only a couple of days before Doors Open Day. Despite this, over 100 people came! Each tour had a group size of 4-5 people and lasted 15-20 minutes. People were given the old architect's drawing of the pool as a 'map' together with a photocopy of the pool opening brochure from 1931. Tour guides started with the group's arrival at the 'slipper bath ticket booth' and escorted them down the long corridor to the men's waiting room. There an attendant would have taken their ticket, given them a towel and taken them to a free bath cubicle. On the tour people learned about the clever architectural features present, and the history and culture of bathing. There are not many intact slipper baths left in the UK attached to swimming pools, or 'bathing establishments', and certainly not of the quality of these.'

BRISTOL TEMPLE MEADS STATION AND TUNNELS

THE ORIGINAL TEMPLE MEADS station was designed by Isambard Kingdom Brunel, the engineer of the Great Western Railway, in 1839-41 incorporating his 7ft-wide broad-gauge line. The 'Tudor-style' building, with its turrets, battlements and buttresses, is still there on the left-hand side of the ramp up to today's station. Inside are the original board room and offices, and in all its magnificence Brunel's train shed – its shallow pitched mock hammer-beam roof spanning 22 metres.

In the 1870s the station was extended and enlarged by Digby Wyatt to accommodate the Bristol & Exeter and the Midland Railways as well as the GWR. He extended Brunel's train shed in a similar if plainer style and designed the adjacent buildings to form most of today's station. A further enlargement to the east by Culverhouse in the 1930s added another five platforms.

Today the Brunel train shed and offices are used as a conference centre and the Digby Wyatt extension for parking cars. However plans are afoot for the latter to become a railway terminal again for the proposed new high-speed electric train to and from London.

Bristol Doors Open Day operates under the nationwide umbrella of Heritage Open Days which provides it with support, national publicity and public liability insurance.

In September 2011 their administrator Nicola Graham visited Bristol and her website blog makes good reading:

'Is anyone afraid of the dark?' It was the last thing we heard before being plunged into blackness. We were underneath Temple Meads Station. It was only 5 seconds of blackness. But it was long enough for the small group of us, blinking together, to gain some understanding of the working conditions of those who forged the tunnels over 100 years before. This is not the beginning of a horror film, rather the final part of a 50-minute tour that I was fortunate enough to gain a place on; just one highlight of the Bristol Open Doors programme. Expertly guided by the Station Managers, Glyn Beck and Nikki Wilcox, it whisks you through the station, hanging its history on visual architectural features: the beautifully wood-panelled offices designed in the 1830s by Brunel, still in use as meeting rooms; the stump of what was once the iron bridge used by passengers to traverse the track, designed in 1870s by Digby Wyatt; the underpass and further platforms, part of Culverhouse's 1930s plans for the station's expansion and in use today.

'And then there are the tunnels: the remains of the original 1830s tracks, nestled in a graveyard of broken glass and vintage lamps and illuminated only by the multiple pinpricks of light from our torches; a V.I.P. air raid shelter reserved for royalty and important members of the public and complete with facilities; a heavy iron 'blast door' abandoned in the curve of a tunnel; iron tracks built for ferrying produce by cart; an abandoned dumb waiter; the remains of 1920s beer cans in the expansive cellars and countless unexplained black corners. It is a coveted tour and it does not disappoint. For all those who wish to experience it, book early!'

(PM) Coveted tours indeed: e-mails and phone calls – hopeful, but in vain – start in January and the tours are fully booked within a couple of weeks of booking actually opening in July.

CLIFTON ROCKS RAILWAY Sion Hill

THE CLIFTON ROCKS RAILWAY was an underground funicular railway, which opened in March 1893, linking the heights of Clifton to the spa of Hotwells and the steamship landing stages on the river. The engineer was Croydon Marks. The tunnel, cut through the limestone cliffs, is 450 feet long and goes a vertical distance of 200 feet at a gradient of about 1 in 2.2. The railway consisted of four cars in two connected pairs, forming two parallel funiculars, each running on 38-inch narrow-gauge tracks. The system was operated by gravity, with water ballast being let into the cars at the top station and out at the bottom, the filled cars pulling up the empty one and an oil- or gas-burning pump returning the water to the top of the system.

The railway was extremely popular – it had 427,492 passengers in its first year. However, it always struggled to be a commercial success and finally closed in October 1934.

A decade later, during the Second World War, blast walls were installed in the tunnel and it was used as an air-raid shelter for local residents, as offices by BOAC, and as a relay station and a (never-used) emergency studio by the BBC. The BBC continued to use parts of the tunnel after the war, but the doors were finally locked in 1960. Over the following years the tunnel was used only for storage by the adjacent Avon Gorge Hotel who currently own most of the site.

In 2005 a dedicated group of volunteers, headed by Peter Davey and Maggie Shapland, was formed to preserve, restore and research the railway. Over the years the Trust has cleared out much of the rubbish that had accumulated in the tunnel and the stations – finding amongst the debris some of the original turnstiles, railings, light fittings, etc, which have been restored and replaced on site.

From 2005, the Rocks Railway has been an extremely popular venue in Doors Open Day – despite the inevitable long queues. Small groups are guided down the steps to stand in the Top Station from where they can look down the track whilst they learn of its history. They then exit through the Avon Gorge Hotel where, on the Day, the Trust has an exhibition about the railway.

Maggie Shapland, Restoration Chair writes:
'That first year, using pick axes and shovels, we started clearing the rubble from the railway lines. We painted the railings and refurbished various artefacts and in September we opened for Doors Open Day for the first time. We opened on the Saturday and the Sunday and had about 3,000 visitors through the doors over those first two days. And each year since we have welcomed up to two thousand people or more over the two days. People come from miles around.

'What is so wonderful is the atmosphere. Everyone loves to hear the history of the site and area, and about the latest research, and come back year after year to see progress. Others come along and want to share their reminiscences of when they travelled on the railway or sheltered there, do University projects on it, or give us family papers relating to the Railway such as the transmitting engineers' wartime training books and a grandfather's log book of all the engineering work he did. Last year the grand daughter of the gang-master of the tunnel construction came to see us as part of her 90th birthday celebrations and I was able to put the family in touch with other family members I had already spoken to. I think the best thing is that everyone has taken the site's story to their hearts.'

THE CONCRETE HOUSE The Ridgeway, Westbury-on-Trym

THE CONCRETE HOUSE, sited in what was in 1934 the outskirts of Bristol, sits on a ridge overlooking the city suburbs. It was designed by the respected firm of Connell Ward and Lucas for an executive of Imperial Tobacco. It is one of the small number of virtually untouched houses left in this country which are examples of the Modern Movement in architecture.

Connell Ward and Lucas brought to Bristol a new and uncompromising contemporary language of architecture reacting against the plethora of late-nineteenth-century and early-twentieth-century 'styles'. The concrete structure used in the Modern Movement allowed for a freer disposition of rooms and walls relating directly to their functions, removing the need for pitched roofs and permitting the extensive use of glazing to maximize sunlight and to relate inside to outside.

The house stood out from its contemporaries in the area. It consists of two overlapping concrete slabs on a north/south axis in a reinforced concrete frame, in-filled with painted concrete walls and finished internally with insulation board used effectively as permanent shuttering for the concrete. At the west end the glazed staircase tower, extending up to a roof terrace, and the curving entrance porch show how the new materials were also used to signify particular functions and to elaborate the composition.

Service spaces occupy the minimally articulated north elevation, and living areas are placed on the extensively glazed south face.

The original exterior colour scheme was not, as now, plain white, but siena yellow walls with plum-red metal window frames. On the ground floor, in the living room, the rigorous orthogonal form of the plan is softened by a curving fireplace, originally plum red to provide a contrast to light-green walls and yellow ceiling. The joinery was a light-stone colour and the sliding doors the same colour as the fireplace. In the adjoining nursery the colour scheme was blue, plum and biscuit.

In August 1994 the Architects Journal *featured a photograph of 'A house at Westbury-on-Trym' to publicise an exhibition on the Modern Movement 1930s practice of Connell Ward & Lucas at the Building Centre in London. It took much asking around but finally I found that it did exist and that it was unaltered. It was lived in by a couple who very much appreciated its classic architectural qualities and who, amazingly, were happy to regularly have what turned out to be some 8-900 enthusiastic people guided through their living rooms on Doors Open Day.*

James Burch, Lecturer in Planning and Architecture at the University of the West of England, who took his students and others, around in 2012 writes:

'When we introduce our first years to The Concrete House they find it both a strange and a familiar building. It is difficult to find it at first attempt – set back from the road and distanced from neighbouring villas that more directly appeal to the students' conventional sense of home. From here there is just a glimpse that persuades them up a tree-lined drive. Journeying within this tunnel, suburbia recedes and fragments of white wall and metal window-frames confirm the students' move into a world of architecture that is new to them. With new ideas: that a house might be 'a machine for living in'? We discuss the sculpted curves that delineate separate car and pedestrian entrance; and the notion that structural expression of column and slab might take a philosophical position about rational truth – yet still tell fibs. Strange new ideas and also something familiar in the interior's hint of television's Poirot, a cat and its most hospitable owner. The perfect student experience'.

The owner comments:
'We wanted to encourage a wider appreciation of this style of architecture. The building society when we applied for a mortgage in the early 70s said the style of architecture was more suited to an airport building than a residence … It was obvious that we didn't get a loan just because they didn't like the look of the house.'

THE EXCHANGE Corn Street

THE EXCHANGE, built at the height of Bristol's trading prosperity, is perhaps the City's finest eighteenth-century building. The work of architect John Wood the Elder and local craftsmen, including the 'ornamental carver', Thomas Paty, it opened for business in 1743. The merchants set up their booths in its large colonnaded court, surrounded by offices let to insurance and other firms. There was no roof over the court – merchants traditionally traded outdoors.

The building's Palladian-style façade has friezes between the tops of the columns representing 'Great Britain and the four quarters of the world with the chief products and Manufacturers of every country'. Similarly inside, over the hall's three entrance doorways, is rococo-plasterwork symbolising Africa, Asia and America.

On the pavement in front of the building are four brass nails on which merchants sealed their grain bargains – which came from the Exchange's predecessor, the Tolzey on the site of the Old Council Office. Two are Elizabethan, two early seventeenth-century.

The Clock has an extra minute-hand showing Bristol Time (ten minutes behind Greenwich Mean Time) – added later to commemorate that before the coming of the railways Bristol had its own time based on the local-standard meridian. Only in 1852 was Greenwich Mean Time adopted.

Significant changes have been made since the Exchange first opened its doors in 1743: the centre was roofed over and an upper-floor added in the 1870s; and a coffee-house and a tavern, situated on either side of the main-entrance, have long gone.

From the 1950s to the end of the 70s the Exchange was used for a variety of functions ranging from pet-shows, weddings and dances to concerts. Today it once again houses a busy market.

Wood's glorious façade, Thomas Paty's delightful plasterwork, and the brass Nails outside are always on show. On Doors Open Day visitors can, in addition, enjoy regular tours organised by the knowledgeable Market Manager, Steve Morris:

'We start in the Exchange Foyer where we highlight some of the interesting features of the building and history.

'We then move onto the first-floor where we discuss the history in a bit more detail:

'The roof, or the fact that the building didn't have a roof initially and that it was only some 130 years later that a roof was inserted, which remained until after the Second World War when owing to blitz damage it was removed and replaced with the existing shallower one.

'The varied uses of the Exchange and in particular its use in the 1960s as a concert venue (at this point I refer to a handbill/flyer which is promoting a Tuesday night club night held at the Exchange and of the Pink Floyd in concert in 1967).

'One of the five houses that Wood built as part of the Exchange and has surviving 1743 features.

'Then up to the second-floor and an opportunity to take a look at the mechanism behind the Exchange Clock which has been in situ since 1822.

'The tours are generally very well received and certainly older Bristolians have fond memories of the Exchange in its various formats.'

'My second Doors Open Day visit.
WELL WORTH IT!'

'A most interesting tour and an excellent guide.'

'Excellent, guide superb, really interesting – put the (original) roof back!'

GLENSIDE HOSPITAL MUSEUM   Blackberry HIll

GLENSIDE HOSPITAL MUSEUM is housed in the Victorian Gothic chapel of the former Bristol Lunatic Asylum. The Asylum (designed by Henry Crisp with later additions by Crisp and George Oatley) opened in 1861, providing much needed in-patient treatment for Bristol's mentally ill.

During the First World War the hospital was requisitioned by the War Office as the Beaufort Military Hospital, housing some 1500 war casualties, but in 1919 it returned to psychiatric care, known first as Bristol Mental Hospital and from 1959 as Glenside Hospital.

In 1994 Glenside Hospital finally closed, becoming home to the University of the West of England's Health & Social Care Faculty. The consultant psychiatrists at the hospital, under the leadership of the late Dr. Donal Early, had for some years been collecting artifacts that illustrated how mental health care had significantly changed over the past century and a half. When the hospital closed, the university authorities gave Dr. Early and his colleagues the use of the chapel to set up as the Hospital Museum of the Mind to promote the better understanding of mental health and the changes and development of its treatment from the 1860s to the late twentieth-century.

Today the Museum continues to be run by volunteers under the leadership now of Dr. Ihsan Mian – also previously a consultant psychiatrist at Glenside. Over the years it has expanded and found new ways of displaying its wide ranging and diverse collection, showing the historical techniques used to treat and contain mental illness.

On display are an array of medications and remedies, E.C.T. machines, a padded cell, a straight jacket, mortuary equipment, ophthalmic instruments, and lifelike displays showing patients in an everyday ward, a sick ward, and an operating theatre. There is even an undercarriage door of a Messerschmitt Bomber that crashed in the grounds in the Second World War.

In addition, following a successful Heritage Lottery application in 2012, the Museum has been organising the recording of memories, experiences and stories from retired staff and patients from Glenside Hospital for future generations.

'A great insight into mental health and the history of Bristol, all displayed in a wonderful old church.'

'Amazing – the passion shown by the museum staff was infectious! Would recommend.'

'What a truly spectacular place! I will be back again.'

'So glad I live in this century – scary stuff!'

'Not as gruesome as I thought it was going to be.'

'So interesting and moving. Hard to believe how times have changed.'

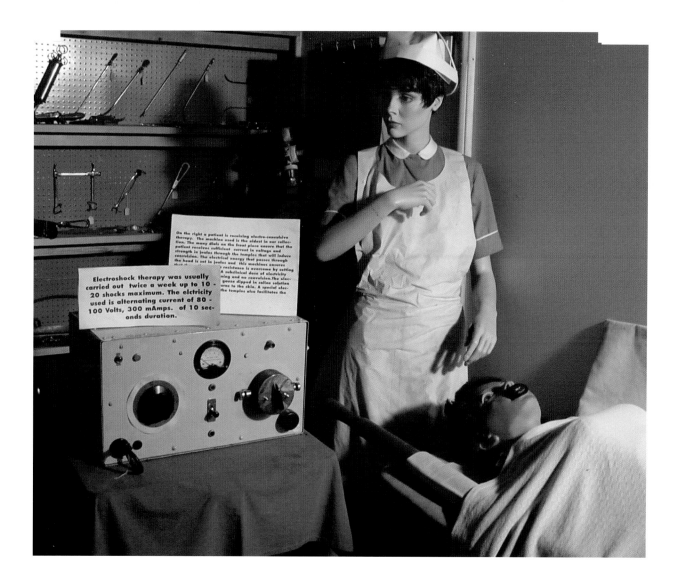

On the right a patient is receiving electro-convulsive therapy. The machine used is the oldest in our collection. The many dials on the front plate ensure that the patient receives sufficient current in voltage and strength in joules through the temples that will induce convulsion. The electrical energy that passes through the head is set in joules and this machines ensures ... resistance is overcome by setting ... ing and no convulsion. The elec... gauze dipped in saline solution ... rms to the skin. A special elec... the temples also facilitates the

Electroshock therapy was usually carried out twice a week up to 10 - 20 shocks maximum. The electricity used is alternating current of 80 - 100 Volts, 300 mAmps. of 10 seconds duration.

HORIZON HOUSE   Deanery Road

HORIZON HOUSE, completed in 2010, is the new national head office of the Environment Agency. Previously its thousand staff were dispersed across five buildings in Bristol and Bath and the EA was keen to bring its employees together. It also wanted to have a building that embodied the environmental principles at the heart of their work, demonstrating that being 'green' makes business sense. Designed by Alec French Architects, every aspect of Horizon House was built with the environment in mind:

- More than 85% of the demolished building that formerly occupied the site was recycled.
- Throughout the building process sustainable building materials, methods and supply chain were used.
- A natural ventilation and cooling system reduces the need for mechanical cooling: fresh air is circulated from under the floor, automated windows provide natural ventilation, 'intelligent lighting systems' reduce energy consumption, and adjustable external blinds help to stop overheating.
- Photovoltaic panels and a solar thermal array convert energy from sunlight into electricity and hot water, and ground source heat pumps provide about 17% of the building's energy needs.
- A rainwater harvesting system reduces mains water consumption by collecting and storing rainwater for use in toilet flushing etc.
- Finally, there are very limited parking facilities to discourage car usage and excellent shower facilities and bike storage to encourage people to cycle and walk to work.

In 2010 it won the Building Research Establishment Environmental Assessment Method (BREEAM) Award for being one of the most environmentally-friendly offices in the UK.

The Environment Agency entered Horizon House as part of Bristol Doors Open Day within months of their move to Bristol in 2011. On their website that year Paul Leinster, Chief Executive of the Environment Agency, wrote:

'We are delighted to welcome the public to Horizon House on Saturday. We hope that the achievements here inspire other organisations to reduce their impact on the environment, and also save money. Visitors will have an opportunity to see how we're reducing our environmental impact. They'll also get an insight into the vital work of the Environment Agency protecting the environment and reducing the risk of flooding.'

Horizon House has proved an extremely popular DOD venue with some 850 visitors in 2011 and even more in 2012 (when the Green Party conference was going on across the road at the Council House).

Hazel Duncan, from their Resources Directorate, writes: 'In 2012 we had: 'Group tours of the building taking in some of the key features of the building and how we work within it sustainably. We took in the views from our balcony while discussing the (sadly out of sight) solar thermal panels and rain water harvesting system that dramatically reduce our water consumption and allow for the heating of our water.

'Tours of our national incident room, with information on the type of events we deal with and how we respond to these, including the recent flooding that had been experienced this summer. They also demonstrated some of the forecasting tools that are used to predict flooding and highlighted how we work in partnership with the Met Office to do this.

'Display and information on Bristol's hidden rivers, looking at the waterways of Bristol and how many of these are underground.

'Demonstration of hydrometry and a telemetry boat, used to measure river flows. The officers also brought with them a rain gauge which visitors could "water".'

M SHED Princes Wharf

BRISTOL'S YOUNGEST MUSEUM – opened in June 2011 – is dedicated to telling the fascinating history of this great city through the objects and stories of the people who have made it what it is today.

The museum is appropriately sited on the water's edge of the Floating Harbour in two rejuvenated early-1950s transit sheds, L & M Shed. Transit sheds – used for storing goods in passage – lined the sides of the former city docks. They were alphabetically labelled: on St. Augustine's Reach was W (today No.1 Harbourside, the Tourist Information Centre & Watershed); U (BSB, McArthurs & Za ZA Bazaar); and V (Pitcher & Piano, 'V Shed' and Bordeaux Quay). Across the water were L and M Shed. Others have been demolished.

L&M were rebuilt post war following bombing damage, and were used for the next twenty years by The Bristol Steam Navigation Company to store a diverse range of goods to and from locations across the world. In the mid-1960s though the city council decided to close the Docks to commercial traffic, in favour of Avonmouth and the run down of shipping facilities on the site began.

In 1977 M Shed re-opened as the Bristol Industrial Museum, with L Shed as a reserve store for museum objects alongside. Many of the dock artefacts became exhibits; four of the iconic dockside cranes had been preserved, thanks to campaigning by a local pressure group; and the Museum service and an enthusiastic team of volunteers took over their maintenance and the running of the steam trains, the 1878 Fairbairn Steam Crane and three historic boats.

In 2006 the Industrial Museum was closed and Lab Architects and designers Event Communications began work to transform M Shed into a twenty-first-century Museum of Bristol. In February 2013, less than two years after its opening, M Shed, the Museum, had its millionth visitor.

Andy King, their Senior Collections Officer, writes:

'In its previous existence as the Industrial Museum, a programme of tours around the museum's reserve stores began, and these have become part of M Shed's regular offer every week. So to give DOD visitors something extra, the tours on the Day are now themed each year to spotlight different elements of the collections that are held there.

'2012 was themed around some of the architectural pieces in the store, including models of the Spectrum building and the stained glass windows from two generations of the Bristol Gas Company's headquarters.

'We also make a point of getting people onto M Shed's working exhibits as much as possible. The first time members of the public visited the dockside crane cabs was on a Doors Open Day in 2002, another pioneering visit that now forms part of the regular programme. We've also regularly opened up the Fairbairn steam crane (a Scheduled Ancient Monument) and our three boats – the Mayflower, *the* Pyronaut *and the* John King *– for visitors to see.*

'And our other major contribution every year is transport, of course. Bristol Harbour Railway's steam trains, which are run by the Museum service, have been a key element of Door Open Day throughout their existence, taking people from the dockside to the westernmost central Bristol sites like the Underfall Yard, Bristol Record Office and Create Centre.'

THE MANSION HOUSE Clifton Down

THE MANSION HOUSE is the official residence of Bristol's Lord Mayor. No Mayor has actually lived here for some 30 years – rather, the grand rooms are used for mayoral entertainment and other civic festivities.

The first Mansion House, in Queen Square, was destroyed in the Bristol Riots of 1831 and was replaced a few decades later by this one in the rather safer heights of Clifton. Designed by the fashionable Victorian architects Charles and Henry Godwin, it was given as a gift to the city in 1874 by one of the city's aldermen, Thomas Proctor.

Bristol has had a Mayor since 1216, a Lord Mayor since 1899 when Queen Victoria granted the city a Lord Mayoralty. Their role is strictly ceremonial and they have no powers in their own right. They are, though, a symbol of Bristol and their role, to quote a previous Lord Mayor, is 'to promote all the good things about the city – promoting the city's identity, encouraging people to believe in the city and seeing opportunities for the city.'

He or she is selected each year by fellow councillors – currently the political parties take it in turns to nominate someone, though the Lord Mayor must be strictly neutral whilst in office.

[As of last year, Bristol also has a Mayor voted for by the electorate of Bristol. The Mayor leads the city council and its full range of services and has ultimate responsibility for the Council's decisions, together with a broader role representing the interests of Bristol's citizens.]

Toni Thompson from the Lord Mayor's Office writes:
'We entered into the scheme (our first year when we had no other commitments) in 2010. As a new participant we were unsure of what was involved – so a baptism by numbers. We had greatly underestimated the interest that we were to generate. We were expecting a couple of hundred visitors and counted through 1623!

'That first year the visitors were organised into tours carried out by members of the Mansion House staff. However, it became evident that the numbers were too many to allow us to do justice to the House or the public.

'So in the following years, we refined the system and instead had a member of staff positioned in each of the exhibition rooms, so that they were able to answer any questions. This system worked well for us and we now use it each DOD.

'The rooms that the public are allowed to view are the public rooms on the ground floor – the large elegant drawing room, the impressive dining room, and the comfortable, bright conservatory which leads into the large front garden; and on the first floor the 3 interconnecting rooms of The Guild of Guardians Suite.

'The Lord Mayor also usually visits us during the day and stays to lend a hand with the "meet and greet".'

The Lord Mayor in 2012/13, Peter Main, adds:
'I am fully supportive of Bristol Doors Open Day. It gave me great pleasure last year to welcome visitors and chat to them about their interest in the House and its history. It was a privilege to listen to their stories about Bristol and to come across people with links to the House and to learn more about our city as a consequence.'

MERCHANTS' HALL The Promenade

BRISTOL IN THE SIXTEENTH CENTURY was England's second City, a position that remained unchallenged for the next two centuries.

The group of Bristol merchants known as the Merchant Venturers received their first royal charter in 1552 which gave members a near monopoly of the city's foreign trade. And early in the 1600s the Society took over the collection of wharfage dues on behalf of the City, reinvesting that income in the port itself which it managed and steadily improved.

In the eighteenth century much of Bristol's wealth came from the slave trade, with some 60% of Bristolians involved both directly and indirectly. The Merchant Venturers Society was not directly involved in the trade – its role was to run the port and to promote trade through Bristol for the benefit of Bristolians – though some individual members were.

At the end of the eighteenth century the Society played a major role in the creation of the Floating Harbour which was completed in 1809. The Society itself never had the capital, or the necessary income, for such a vast undertaking and with the setting up of the Bristol Docks Company most of the Society's responsibilities for the port ended.

Thereafter, the Merchants have concentrated upon their ever-increasing responsibilities in education and the care of the elderly – historic roles that predate that first royal charter of 1552.

Today's Merchants' Hall in Clifton overlooks The Promenade and combines two grand semi-detached Victorian mansions acquired after the destruction of the original hall, in central Bristol, during the Blitz.

On Doors Open Day tours, led by Merchants, take groups of visitors through the Reception Room where the Quarterly Hall meetings of the Society are held; along the hall where the early charters are on show; into the Dining Room with its long table, full-length portraits and grand chandeliers; upstairs past an intriguing one-handed clock and some very fine paintings of the Avon Gorge; finally into the Committee Room, with its pictures of past Treasurers, where the Standing Committee and the many sub-committees of the Society meet.

Francis Greenacre, Merchant Venturer, writes:
'The Merchant Venturers have played a major role in Bristol for five hundred years and that fascinating story can best be told and illustrated within Merchants' Hall. But we did not open our doors simply to tell that story. Our present role in education and the care of the elderly, our management of charitable trusts and our desire to enhance the quality of life for all in the Greater Bristol area can be handicapped by the inevitable suspicion that any such body attracts. Doors Open Day is to our own advantage. It makes our job easier and we have much to share.'

'As someone who has lived in Bristol for 30 years, it was intriguing to see inside the headquarters of an organisation that has been somewhat shrouded in mystery, and yet has such influence in the City. Despite their links to Bristol's slave trading heritage, they have now clearly dedicated themselves to using their wealth to make a difference, in developing education and the care of older people, which is heartening.'

THE OLD COUNCIL HOUSE AND BRISTOL REGISTRY OFFICE Corn Street

THE GREEK REVIVAL-STYLE building that houses the Bristol Registry Office provides elegant surroundings for those wishing to effect a civil marriage or partnership, or become naturalised citizens – or those wanting a space for a special occasion.

The original two-storey neo-Classical building is the work of Sir Robert Smirke, also the architect of St. George's Brandon Hill and of the British Museum.

It was built between 1824-7 as the city's Council House – replacing a previous one in Small Street. The fine Regency-style room at the top of the grand stairs, with its richly decorated ceiling and circular lantern and now known as The Lantern Room, is Smirke's original Council Chamber. The Bristol Room was his Treasurer's Office. In 1828 the building was extended to the side in order to house a Magistrates' Court by R.S. Pope and G. Dymock, and in 1889 a larger Council Chamber was added at the back.

As local government powers expanded in the mid-twentieth century, the City Council found they again needed larger premises. In the early 1950s they moved out to the new Council House on College Green and the vacated building became the Magistrates' Courts. Then in 1996 the Magistrates too moved out as new Law Courts were built in Small Street. For several years the Old Council House remained unoccupied looking for a new owner and use.

The Old Council House first participated in Doors Open Day in 1998.

It had been standing empty for a couple of years and the City Valuer saw it as an opportunity to spread the news that this important building was on the market. For the next six years up to 2,500 visitors came on DOD each year.

Finally, with the development of Cabot Circus and the sale of the Quakers Friars Registry Office there, the Council was able to find a use. In 2007, following restoration and refurbishment, the Bristol Registry Office moved from its previous home in Quakers Friars.

For three years from 2008 the Registration team continued to participate in DOD – opening on the Sunday to avoid weddings. It wasn't easy – each year the usher on Saturdays found himself having to fend off potential visitors who had not realised they were only open for ceremonies. And as Shirley Kirby the Registration Manager wrote in 2008:

'Open on Sunday due to weddings on Saturday, only to have the city centre closed to traffic on Sunday due to the half-marathon being held. Still we managed 450 visitors!

'We had displays of photographs showing the 'before and after' renovation, old historic photographs of the building and photographs of the cells (closed to DOD visits since renovation, to people's disappointment).

'The family history, history of registration and other historical records were of particular interest.'

Sadly, recently, the public spending cuts have hit and they have felt unable to take part in DOD.

THE RED LODGE WIGWAM   Park Row

BEHIND THE WALL of the garden of the sixteenth-century Red Lodge – with its re-created Tudor knot garden and herbaceous borders of plants that could have been found in a Jacobean English garden – stands the surprising sight of a twentieth-century version of a sixteenth-century tithe barn. Known as The Wigwam, it was designed c.1920 by C.F.W. Dening (a Bristol Savage and the architect of Bristol South Slipper Baths q.v.) as the meeting place and gallery for the Bristol Savages, a club for artists and art-lovers.

In 1918 Alderman James Fuller Eberle, Chairman of the Museum and Art Gallery Committee of Bristol Corporation and a prominent Bristol Savage, had learnt that the Red Lodge was likely to come up for sale. Dealers throughout the country had been patiently waiting for years for the Lodge to come onto the market in order that they could secure its rich interior fittings for the benefit of American clients. It was, though, an inopportune time to ask that the purchase be publicly funded. Alderman Eberle, confident that friends would support him, bought the property himself. He had two purposes in mind – to donate the last of the sixteenth-century mansions in the City to Bristolians, and to make a new home for the Bristol Savages.

The Society was founded in 1904, when the concept of the 'noble savage' was seen as something to aspire to, and the Native American culture still plays a part in the Bristol Savages' traditions. When they meet in the Red Lodge's 'wigwam' each member wears on their lapel either a red, blue or green feather – red for artists, blue for entertainers (singers, instrumentalists, raconteurs etc.) and green for lay-members. The feathers are pinned on with a badge made from a vintage US five-cent piece, first issued in 1913, depicting a composite American Indian profile from models Chief John Big Tree, a Seneca, Chief Two Moons, a Cheyenne, and Chief Iron Tail, a Sioux.

Jeffrey Mason, a Bristol Savage, writes:
'Bristol Savages was founded in 1904 by Ernest Ehlers, Arthur Wilde Parsons and other artist friends meeting informally at each other's studios to paint and enjoy good companionship. After sojourns at a room at the Royal Hotel on College Green and a room over a gunsmith's shop in Corn Street, the growing group established itself in 1907 in an earlier 'Wigwam' at Brandon Cottage, owned by James Fuller Eberle. In 1920 they moved into their current Wigwam in the Red Lodge garden.

'By now, there were entertainment and lay members as well as artists and a traditional Wednesday evening was well established.

'That tradition continues today, with artists meeting weekly to paint a two-hour sketch – the subject nominated by the Chairman for the evening – before joining their colleagues for the evening's entertainment of vocal and instrumental music, magic, poetry and prose.

'The new Wigwam became not only the meeting place of Bristol Savages but also a home for their large collection of artefacts and paintings, which were the gifts of many members and friends and have come from around the world, this being a tradition that has continued since the Bristol Savages moved into the Wigwam in 1920. Gifts include three seventeenth-century fireplaces, three oak doors from the same period, four corbels supporting the Minstrel Gallery at the rear of the building and many other items.'

REDCLIFFE CAVES   Phoenix Wharf

HIDDEN BEHIND SMALL and inconspicuous locked doors in the cliffs on the Floating Harbour are Redcliffe Caves. They penetrate for an acre or more into the red sandstone and are known to stretch nearly as far as the General Hospital. It is also possible that the caves once linked up with the crypt of St. Mary Redcliffe.

These intriguing caves owe their existence to the pick axe, rather than natural elements, and date from medieval times. In 1346 a hermit, John Sparkes, occupied part of the caves praying for his benefactor, Thomas Berkeley, whose family then owned the Redcliffe and Bedminster areas of Bristol. Between the mid-seventeenth and nineteenth centuries the caves expanded fast, as sand was extracted from the cliffs for the making of glass bottles, something the Redcliffe area was once famous for. The sand was also used for ships' ballast and to scatter on the floor of local pubs.

Excavation stopped in the early nineteenth-century when Bristol's last glass manufactory closed, but until the late nineteenth century the caves continued to be used as storage.

There are inevitably many local myths about them with tales of smuggling and hidden treasure and darker stories of African slaves being imprisoned in the caves. In reality, the only slaves that arrived in Bristol were as personal servants to rich merchants – the rest were shipped direct from Africa to the Americas. Spanish and French prisoners of war were however held in the caves in the 1740s.

In the twentieth-century the caves came into use again – providing shelter for Redcliffe citizens during the dark days of the Bristol Blitzes between 1940 and 1942. But in the 1950s the doors were firmly locked and the caves left unused, save for the occasional filming of a television episode.

The caves have for the past 19 years consistently been one of the most popular Doors Open Day venues, with each year between 3-4,000 visitors. In 1995 – its first year – it had over 6,000.

Visitors to the caves walk along dark passages, past the roughly hewn stone 'pillars' and blocked off caverns. One such used to lead to the late-eighteenth-century lead-shot tower, demolished in 1968, – the hot metal became spherical falling down the shaft into water and was very suitable for gun cartridges. Elsewhere brick shafts intrude from the Georgian terraces above.

We first tried to get access in 1994, the first year of DOD, but the City Council officer in charge wrote back: 'I regret to inform you that access cannot be permitted for Health and Safety reasons; and in particular:

> *the Caves extend over several hundred metres and have been described as resembling a rabbit warren.*

> *there is no lighting or signing in the tunnels, which are damp and occasionally dangerous under foot.'*

Refusing to be put off, we lobbied other officers and by the following year a solution had been found: Axbridge Caving Group (ACG under the leadership of Alan Gray) was granted a special licence, first to explore the caves and then specifically to supervise the public on Doors Open Day.

It is a mutually beneficial arrangement:

DOD visitors are supervised by highly experienced cavers who are very knowledgeable about Redcliffe Caves and their history. The only requirement we have each year is that the public should wear stout shoes and bring a torch. In turn ACG sell their guidebooks and, if necessary, hire out torches to those without one.

'The highlight for both of us [mother and child] was the trip around Redcliffe Caves, in fact so much we went round twice. Nothing beats the sheer atmosphere of exploring this maze of caverns, dead-ends and passages by torchlight.'

ROYAL FORT HOUSE   Tyndall Avenue

ROYAL FORT HOUSE, built on the site of a Civil War fortification 1758-61 – probably by James Bridges – has one of the finest eighteenth-century interiors in Bristol. Rooms of strict Palladian proportions set off exuberant rococo plasterwork by Thomas Stocking and stone-carving and rococo wood-carving by Thomas Paty. The walls and ceilings, even the stairway, are decorated with elaborate rococo plaster decoration, with vines, birds, squirrels, a fox.

It was the home from 1760-90 of Thomas Tyndall, member of a wealthy Bristol family – their wealth acquired over many years through trade with Africa and the West Indies – and Tyndall descendants continued to live there until 1916 when the house and the land immediately surrounding was sold to the University.

Thomas Tyndall during his life time had bought up the leases of surrounding estates, but after his death in 1790 much of the surrounding land was sold to a syndicate for housing development. The scheme however foundered with the bankruptcy of the syndicate in the Great Crash of 1793, brought about by the financial panic consequent on the war with France. The land reverted to the family, and the damage to the landscape done by the preliminary quarrying excavations was later repaired by Sir Humphry Repton.

Today the building houses Bristol University's Institute of Advanced Studies.

Repton's original drive and planting around the house have recently been reinstated by the University and in 2009 as part of their centenary celebrations, the Danish artist Jeppe Hein was commissioned to produce the mirrored labyrinth of seventy-six vertical mirrored plates that can be seen in the garden.

Diane Thorne, the University's Events Officer, writes:
'Every year, during Doors Open Day, Royal Fort House opens its doors to the public. Visitors are invited inside to view the spectacular rooms which include:

'the Entrance Hall – which features decorative brackets on the wall whose original purpose was to carry lamps and the eighteenth-century brass floor-heating inlets,

'the Dining Room – showcasing decorative rococo plaster work by Thomas Stocking,

'the Staircase Hall – spectacular rococo stucco plaster work on the walls by Thomas Stocking and a magnificent Edwardian chandelier hanging over the staircase,

'the Library and Drawing/Withdrawing Rooms.

'Guided historical tours are available throughout the day'.

'The plasterwork on the ceiling and walls is beautiful.'

'The tour of the building was excellent.'

'The beautiful architecture and the unusual rooms (carvings etc).
The Installation in the grounds.'

THE ROYAL WEST OF ENGLAND ACADEMY and the SCHOOL OF ART Queen's Road

THE WEST OF ENGLAND ACADEMY was Bristol's first art gallery when it opened in 1858 – the Royal nomenclature was granted by King George V in 1914.

Its exterior was designed in Italian renaissance-style by architect J.H. Hirst and its interior by Charles Underwood; and then just over 50 years later the grand exterior flights of steps were removed and yet another architect, S.S. Reay, modified the interior entrance area.

The Academy's large classical-style gallery is on the first-floor of the building, entered through the main door and up the stairs. On the ground-floor below it, but entered through the right-hand side of the building, is the School of Art, a practical space designed for use by art students and complementing the more ornate structure of the RWA above.

The huge School of Art Life Room matches the main gallery above and with its north light, is a formally designed space for drawing.

Both parts of the building participate in Doors Open Day. The RWA offers free entry into its current exhibition – numbers vary according to the show, but in 2012 with an exhibition titled Unnatural Natural History, an artistic exploration of an alternative world, they had 1100 visitors.

The School of Art encourages people to see the building as it is in use and over the 13 years it has featured in Doors Open Day, has offered a range of art-school activities for both adults and children.

Dr. Oliver Kent, tutor at the School of Art, writes:

'Visitors can participate in life-classes (with a clothed model) and screen-printing activities, both very popular. When Habitat was still open, you would see people leaving the school carrying their prints and heading straight into the shop to buy frames! With the help of our staff, and the children who are always the best ice-breakers, visitors rapidly form an industrious community, drawing in the Life Room.

'We also do guided tours for those who would like them and are happy to discuss the history of the building, art education and debate the merits of Damien Hirst, Tracey Emin, or the Arnolfini!

'Current students like to use it as an opportunity to bring parents and friends – and it is always nice to see their pride in the place. One of the unexpected consequences of DOD has been the return of ex-students from before and after the war, curious to see how the place has changed or to tell us about their time here. This year one such student had last used the life room in 1952. We made her very welcome and our drawing tutor Kate got her working again. She asked for a traditional 'donkey' drawing stool to sit on as she had in the 50s and one was duly found.

'Others have told us about fire-watching on the roof during the Second World War – during the war the building housed various organisations including the Bristol Aeroplane Company and the U.S. Army – and other memories.'

ST. JAMES' PRIORY CHURCH   Whitson Street

ST. JAMES' IS BRISTOL'S oldest surviving building, originally a part of the Benedictine Priory of St. James, founded c.1129. Initially the monks' church, in the fourteenth-century it became a parish church for the surrounding population. The monastic buildings were sold in the dissolution of the monasteries and became a private residence – but the Parish Church continued unchanged for over four hundred years.

Then in the early 1980s, the number of its parishioners having severely dwindled as a result of both the blitz and slum clearance, the church was declared redundant. For the next decade it remained empty, unused and increasingly derelict.

In 1987 as part of their 250-year celebrations the residents of Kingsdown, part of the Outer Parish of St. James', cleaned out the nave and for a week held an extremely successful community play in the church, drawing attention to its plight. It was another year or more though before the church was finally put on the market by the Church Commissioners. It attracted several hopeful buyers – one wishing to convert it into offices, another to use it as an extension to the Bus Station. To general relief these offers were unsuccessful.

Finally in 1993, to widespread approval, the Little Brothers of Nazareth applied to set up the St. James' Priory Project. The Brothers offer support to vulnerable people especially those with a history of substance dependency and mental illness. Today, the church, once more Catholic, continues to provide vital inner city social care – whilst at the same time offering a haven of serenity and peace in the heart of the city.

The building itself – already in bad condition after years of neglect – continued to deteriorate until in 2006 the Little Brothers gained HLF funding for restoration under the direction of architects, Ferguson Mann. Internally and externally the stonework, plasterwork and paintwork were all restored to their previous glory.

In 2011 St. James' opened its doors again to the public.

In Doors Open Day that year Rob Harding, a volunteer, sought out other helpers to research the histories of the names recorded on the church's memorials. He wrote:

'When the St James' Priory Family History Research Group started, little was known beyond what was inscribed on the memorials themselves. Slowly they are uncovering the histories of the people commemorated – slave traders, plantation owners and Bristol sugar house operators as well as Lord Mayors, brewers and manufacturers. With regard to the names recorded on the parish First World War memorial, we now know where the men lived before enlisting, what work they did and details of their families.'

On Doors Open Day the Priory Trust also opens the immediately adjacent Jacobean Church House. Restoration work included repairing the fine Jacobean decorated plaster ceiling in the front room and removing paint from two statues on either side of the overmantle above the fireplace. 'They were camouflaged with a layer of nasty modern brown paint' said the conservator 'but paint conservation work revealed them to be a lush pair of rouged, cornucopia-clutching seventeenth-century over-painted ladies.' Their origin is unknown, but it is thought they represent not medieval saints, but the handmaidens of the Roman Goddess Abundia, the personification of abundance, prosperity and good fortune.

'Then on to the peace and dignity of St. James' Church, where the humbling experience of discovering the work being done by the Little Brothers of Nazareth in helping the homeless was enhanced by the absolute silence being observed by all the visitors.'

ST. JOHN'S ON THE WALL   Broad Street

THE MEDIEVAL CHURCH of St. John's sits on what is left of the City's ancient enclosing wall, at the bottom of Broad Street. The first mention of a church on this site is in 1174 AD, but today the oldest part of the present building, the crypt, dates back to the early fourteenth-century. The rest was rebuilt, between 1380 and 1400, thanks to the generosity of rich Bristol merchant and Mayor, Walter Frampton, whose fine tomb, flanked by angels, can be seen inside.

As well as its unique position astride the one remaining gate in the City's thirteenth-century wall, the church has Bristol's only remaining medieval spire. The gaily-painted statues in the niches above the carriageway through, possibly seventeenth-century, are reputed to be Brennus and Bellinus, the mythical founders of Bristol. The coats of arms, above and below the statues, are those of King Charles II, the City of Bristol and the Merchant Venturers.

Built into the outside wall of the church (but at one time on the inside) is St. John's conduit, to which water from a spring on Brandon Hill had been piped since 1376 – although sadly it has recently stopped flowing.

The main body of St. John's is entered up steps off Broad Street. The panelled pulpit dates from the fifteenth century, the pews and font date from the seventeenth century and the seven fine painted panels of the saints are possibly by an eighteenth-century Dutch artist.

Below is the church's rib-vaulted crypt, entered by a small wooden door and down stone steps from Nelson Street. Here is an alabaster tomb thought to belong to Thomas Rowley, Sheriff of Bristol, who died in 1478 and who has a brass to his memory in the church. Was this where Chatterton got the name for his supposed 'fifteenth-century priest' when he was creating his poems three centuries later? This Thomas Rowley though had a wife and many sons and daughters – and you can still see, despite the all-pervading gloom, their figures on the side of the tomb.

Having lost its congregation over the years the building is now cared for by the Churches Conservation Trust who also care for two other Doors Open Day venues, St. Paul's and St. Thomas. St. Paul's is now the home of Circomedia Circus School, but St. Thomas, as with St. John's, remains generally unused.

'Very peaceful away from the City hustle and bustle. A great opportunity to visit.'

'Lived here all my life – first time visited – fascinating.'

'Did not know this place existed. Amazing.'

'Have longed to see inside for many years and am now so impressed – what a wonderful heritage.'

ST. MARY REDCLIFFE CHURCH   Redcliffe Way

'THE FAIREST, GOODLIEST and most famous parish church in our realm' supposedly said Queen Elizabeth I of this master-piece of Gothic architecture when she visited the city in 1574.

From the outside, the church she saw then was somewhat different from the church today. The spire had been struck by lightning in 1446 leaving only a tower-like stump and the spire we so admire today is a Victorian replica. At nearly 300 feet it is one of the tallest in the country.

The main structure of the church, together with its spectac-ularly decorated interior, is the work of the thirteenth to fifteenth centuries, building on the site of a twelfth-century Saxon church, the masons rebuilding and extending it in ever grander and more decorated style. The hexagonal north porch leading to the main entrance is early fourteenth-century. Richly deco-rated in intricate foliage with tiny hiding figures, it intriguingly has what appear to be Islamic or Indian influences. The more restrained inner section is of the early thirteenth century.

Within the church the spectacular decorated surfaces and intricate carving work of those early masons continues. Its high narrow vaults are richly decorated with more than twelve hundred superb painted roof bosses mostly naturalistic foliage, sometimes figures, sometimes grotesques – the full detail only fully appreciated with binoculars.

The fine tombs and monuments include, among others, those in the south transept of William Canynges II, five times mayor of Bristol, who funded much of the fifteenth-century church; and in the north nave that of seventeenth-century Admiral William Penn, the Parliamentarian naval commander – his armour on show above – whose Quaker son founded Pennsylvania. Also in the north nave, close to Penn's monu-ment is a large curved whalebone – presented by John Cabot as thanks for his successful voyage across the Atlantic in 1497; and a wooden, painted statue of Queen Elizabeth I, which came from Bristol Grammar School and is thought to have been made for her 1574 visit.

The main body of St. Mary Redcliffe is of course open to the general public throughout the year. Venues like that, however, are expected to provide special access to generally unavailable spaces.

Pat Terry, the Parish Administrator, writes:

'On Open Doors Day we offer:

'Trips to the Bell Chamber – the church has one of the finest peals of bells in the country. Ringers give a demonstration and offer people the chance to try for themselves. The oldest bell (the eleventh) was cast in 1622, the newest (the eighth) in February 2013 replacing one cast in 1768, now sadly out of tune.

'Trips to the Chatterton Room – an ancient muniment room, historically the ancient strong room of the church, where the records and treasures of the parish were originally stored. This is the document room where in the 1760s Thomas Chatterton claimed to have discovered some medieval manuscripts with poetry written by the fifteenth-century monk, Thomas Rowley – in reality created by himself.

'Trips to the roof – one of the finest views of Bristol.'

ST. VINCENT'S WORKS   Silverthorne Lane

THE DELIGHTFUL CRENELLATED 'Gothic castle' in Silverthorne Lane was designed by R.M. Drake in the 1880s as the administrative offices for John Lysaght's Iron Works. Lysaght was the highly successful manufacturer of corrugated iron and pre-fabricated buildings. His firm's products – which included houses, farm buildings, railway stations, and even churches – were exported all round the world and particularly to Australia where they were especially popular among the early settlers. In those gold-rush years prospectors would apparently arrive in Melbourne with a Lysaght Home in the ship's hold, packed and numbered in a ready-to-assemble kit.

John Lysaght may have manufactured mainly rather utilitarian material, but his administrative offices were in total Victorian contrast: in the atrium a dome of golden tiles decorated with a fleet of boats ranging from an Egyptian dhow to a British battle cruiser, Doulton tiles covering every available wall space, elaborate handrails with snarling gryphons, central heating radiators with pillar pipes shaped like classic Doric columns.

Today St. Vincent's Works is the headquarters of an equally successful international engineering firm: Garrad Hassan, the world's largest renewable energy consultancy, experts in on-shore and off-shore wind, wave, tidal and solar sectors.

The firm bought the sadly neglected building in 2000. It had been empty for two years and was much in need of restoration and renovation.

The owner's wife, Emma, writes: 'I had visited St. Vincent's at a Doors Open Day in the early 1990s and been so excited by the building. I recognised Andrew's description of a potential new office immediately. The family were therefore committed to reopening to the public, and readily agreed following an approach from Bristol DOD in 2001.

'Over the years the Garrads and Hassans, with help from staff, have thoroughly enjoyed showing people round this amazing building; and my children have been very much involved over the years both as guides and as refreshment organisers. Although they are now grown up they still return to Bristol, if time allows, for Doors Open Day.

'On the Day we have seen many old employees of both John Lysaght and Blagdon Packaging, all with a story to tell – and touchingly an elderly lady who had walked past the building every day as a child on her way to school and called it her 'fairy castle'. She had never been inside the building and was absolutely delighted to be there at our first open day.'

UNDERFALL YARD Cumberland Road

THE UNDERFALL YARD AREA, together with the nearby Cumberland Basin lock system, are key features of Bristol's Floating Harbour, created in 1804-09 to the design of engineer William Jessop. The natural course of the tidal River Avon was dammed at the site of the Underfall Yard with the Cumberland Basin locks cut through the adjacent water meadows. The New Cut to the south was excavated to create a tidal river bypass and the non-tidal Floating Harbour was formed, remaining largely unaltered today.

The new dam incorporated a weir, the Overfall, and sluices to maintain the dock water level. Over the following decades the build-up of silt proved to be a problem in the Harbour and in 1832, I.K. Brunel, then the dock engineer, recommended improvements to the operation of the sluices.

In the 1890s the Overfall was finally replaced with three shallow sluices and one deep mud-scouring sluice for silt disposal. The shallow sluices provide for the adjustment of the docks' water level according to weather conditions. The new system, powered by a central hydraulic pumping station which also provided power to the locks, bridges and cranes, was called the Underfall.

The sluices remain in operation today, although now computer-controlled and individually powered. The system is also an important element in Bristol's flood control systems.

Throughout the 1880s and 1890s the area around the Underfall sluices, the Underfall Yard, was gradually reclaimed and developed as a maintenance and dredging base by the dock's engineer, Girdlestone.

Until about 1910, all maintenance work for the City and the Avonmouth & Portishead dock systems was carried out at Underfall Yard. Then after a new base was established at Avonmouth in 1910, it served the City Docks only, until its closure to commercial shipping in 1975.

Underfall Yard is a popular destination on Doors Open Day and in 2012 they counted some 800 visitors.

Since 1975 the maintenance requirements of the harbour have further reduced. Where previously the Yard was home to shipwrights, dredger men, mechanical and electrical engineers, riggers, blacksmiths, builders and divers, today far fewer people with such skills are needed. Whilst Underfall Yard continues to be the base for the small council maintenance team still required, it is now home to boat builders, rope workers, composite-fibre craftsmen and workers with other related skills.

In one of the large sheds and in the Pump House visitors can see some of the large machines from Girdlestone's time actually operating and learn about their historical function. In the other sheds they can watch modern boats being built and the blacksmith and other craftsmen displaying their skills. On the Slip they can see harbour boats being maintained.

'Love that there's still a working part of the harbour – real, not pretty – still got the smells.'

'Fantastic, historic but still actively a working yard.'

'Nice that there's traditional activity in an urban harbour area still active in a historical way right in the centre of Bristol.'

WILLS MEMORIAL BUILDING Queen's Road

THE NEO-GOTHIC Wills Memorial Building was commissioned by George and Henry Wills of the Wills Tobacco Company as a memorial to their father, Henry Overton Wills III.

It was Henry Overton Wills III's pledge of £100,000, followed by others in the city, that had made the foundation of the University possible and in 1909 he became its first chancellor.

The sons wanted an 'impressive main building on a conspicuous site' and the Wills Memorial Building by architect Sir George Oatley certainly fulfils that brief. Its massive 215-feet high 'Gothic Perpendicular-style' tower at the top of Park Street dominates the Bristol skyline. The impressive Entrance Hall is 75 feet high with double-staircases to the first-floor and Gothic fan-vaulting on the ceiling. The Great Hall, a magnificent 100-feet-long room, can seat a thousand people for graduation ceremonies and other important occasions.

The building was opened by King George V in June 1925, building work having been halted in the First World War. There was a week of festivities to celebrate 'Bristol's Royal Week' and the city centre was decorated with brightly coloured flags, bunting and streamers. Wills Memorial Building was open to the public for the two days after the opening and it was reckoned that 50,000 people went round it in just one day. (The most we have recorded in DOD for Wills is 3,552 in 2008!)

The tower's bell, Great George, is so named in honour of the three Georges: King George V, Sir George Oatley and Sir George Wills. It is the fourth largest bell in England.

The University's Events Officer, Diane Thorne, writes:
'As well as the Entrance Hall and the Great Hall visitors on Doors Open Day can see:

'The Council Chamber: the room originally used for meetings of the University Council. On the longest wall are the shields of benefactors of the University.

'The Library: The oldest part is 100-feet long and has a beautiful sixteenth-century-style plaster ceiling. A bust of Sir George Oatley can be seen near the entrance.

'The Tower Tours: Visitors are invited to take a guided tour past the 9½-ton bell, Great George, to the top of the Wills Memorial Building Tower, which gives spectacular views all over Bristol.

'Research Exhibition: Visitors are given a taste of the research and teaching that goes on at the University whilst visiting our interactive exhibition. These exhibits showcase research from nano-science and biodiversity to oceanography and palaeontology. The exhibition gives visitors the chance to talk to our researchers, uncover new insights and make their own discoveries. Many of the activities are hands-on and suitable for children and adults of all ages.'

'I have lived in Bristol for over 30 years and I have never been in this building. Thank you.'

'The Tower Tour is spectacular – I can't believe Park Street looks flat from up there!!'

'Brilliant [research exhibition], enjoyed a very informative and learning experience for the children and me.'

DOD 12 tweets from @GreatGeorgeWMB, the Bell,
'[16:00] 'Absolutely exhausted while people look, poke and prod. I had a couple of nice hugs though – thank you.'

NEW VENUES EACH YEAR

1994
29 Queen Square
35 Corn St
Bristol Cathedral, College Green
Bristol Museum & Art Gallery, Queen's Rd
Bristol United Press, Temple Way
Clifton RC Cathedral, Clifton Park
Colston's Almshouses, St Michael's Hill
Council House, College Green
Create Centre, Smeaton Rd
Eastern Orthodox Church, University Rd
Engineers' House, The Promenade
Exchange, Corn St
Georgian House, Gt George St
High St Vaults
John Wesley's Chapel, Horsefair
Marketing Centre, Avon St
New Law Courts, Broad St
No.1 Bridewell St
Quakers Friars, Broadmead
Red Lodge, Park Row
RNIB Vision Care, Stillhouse Lane
Royal Fort House, Tyndall Ave
St. James' Priory, Whitson St
St. Mary Redcliffe, Redcliffe Way
St. Nicholas/BARAS, St Nicholas St
St. Vincent's Works/Blagdon Packaging
Underfall Yard, Cumberland Rd
Wills Memorial Building, Queen's Rd

1995
All Saints Church, Pembroke Rd
Ashton Court, Ashton Park
At-Bristol, Harbourside
Blaise Castle House Museum
Brew House, Kings Weston
Clifton College, Clifton Rd
Concrete House, The Ridgeway
Industrial Museum, Princes Wharf
Kings Weston Roman Villa
Lord Mayor's Chapel, College Green
Redcliffe Caves, Phoenix Wharf
Redland Chapel
Royal West of England Academy

St. Michael's Church, St Michael's Hill
Stratford Mill, Blaise
Unitarian Meeting House, Brunswick Square
Wessex Water / Bristol Sewage treatment

1996
Architecture Centre, Narrow Quay
Black Castle Chapel, Bath Rd
Christ Church, Broad St
Kings Weston House, Kings Weston Lane
Lloyds Bank, Corn St
Merchant Venturers House (U of B), Park Row
RAC Supercentre, Bradley Stoke
St. John's on the Wall, Broad St

1997
Castle Park Vaults
Central Library, College Green
CLIC House, Fremantle Square
Edward Everard entrance, Broad St
Green House, Hereford St
NatWest, Avon St
QEH School, Berkeley Place
Smiles Brewery, Colston St
Spectrum Building, Bond St
Spike Island (ex Art Space)
SunLife HQ, Stoke Gifford
Victoria Rooms, Queen's Rd

1998
Bristol Grammar School
Bristol Old Vic, King St
Broadmead Baptist Church
Charles Wesley's House, Charles St
Fosters Almshouses, Colston St
Lloyds Canons House, Harbourside
Old Council House, Corn St
Old Stock Exchange, St Nicholas St
Red Lodge Wigwam, Park Row
Temple Church, Victoria St

1999
Harvey's Wine Cellars, Denmark St
Meeting House, Lewins Mead

MOD, Abbey Wood
Nat West, Corn St
Old Baptist College, Woodland Rd
Old Police Station, Jacob's Wells Rd
Tobacco Factory, Raleigh Rd

2000
Armada House, Telephone Avenue
Bristol Magistrates Court, Nelson St
Bristol School of Art
Empire Museum & Brunel tours, Temple Meads
Fairbairn Steam Crane, Wapping Wharf
Muller Museum, Cotham Park
St. Nicholas Almshouses, King St
Synthetic Chemistry, Cantocks Close

2001
Bishopsworth Manor House
City of Bristol, College Green Centre
Compact Power, Avonmouth
Henbury Manor, Henbury
St. Thomas Church, St Thomas St
The Point, Wapping Wharf

2002
Bristol Blue Glass
City Learning Centre Brislington
City Learning Centre Monks Park
Cotham School
Fosters Rooms
Pierian Centre
Temple Quay B&W
Temple Quay DLTR
UWE Architecture
UWE Education

2003
Bristol Hippodrome
Bristol Record Office
Temple Quay – Osborne Clarke
St. Paul's Clifton
St. Stephen's

FUNDERS AND SUPPORTERS over the years 1994-2013

Alder King
Alec French Architects
Architecture Centre Bristol *
Arnolfini
Arts Council
Arup
Avon County Council
Beaufort
Brandon Hill Communications
Bristol Chamber of Commerce & Initiative / Business West
Bristol City Council
Bristol Civic Society
Bristol Cycling Campaign
Bristol [Evening] Post
Bristol Ferry Boat Co.
Bristol Property Agents Association
Bristol Tour Open Bus
Bristol United Press
BT
Building a Better Bristol

Burges Salmon
City Line
CompuAdd
Crosby
First City Line
GWR fm
HBG Construction / BAM
Heritage Open Days National Partnership
Investment South West Arts
JT
Montage
Nat West Life Assurance
Skanska
South West Electricity Board
SunLife
The Loop Agency
The Mail Marketing Group
The Tourist Information Centre, Harbourside
Trimedia
Under the Sky Urban Renewal

* Building on Bristol Doors Open Day, the Architecture Centre has recently launched Bristol Opening Doors which provides smart-phone apps, printed walking trails, and teaching and learning resources to several of the Doors Open Day venues, enabling residents, visitors and schools to explore the interiors of the buildings throughout the year.

Of those covered in detail here: Bristol Heart Institute, Bristol Old Vic, Bristol Temple Meads, Horizon House, The Old Council House, St.James' Priory, The Exchange and Wills Memorial Building are all included.
See: www.BristolOpeningDoors.org for details and other buildings they have done.

The Opening Doors project has been funded by the Heritage Lottery Fund Heritage programme, with additional support from the Bristol Building Preservation Trust, Bristol City Council and the Drake Trust.

THE AUTHOR

PENNY MELLOR has been actively involved in Bristol Doors Open Day since its initiation.

Her publications include *Kingsdown: Bristol's Vertical Suburb* and *A Kingsdown Community*.

Also available from Redcliffe Press:

Open Doors: Bristol's hidden interiors

Text by Tim Mowl and photographs by Stephen Morris

This elegant introduction to 45 Doors Open venues complements *Inside Bristol*. It contains many buildings not featured in the current book, including Bishopsworth Manor House, Bristol Blue Glass Workshop, Bristol Royal Hospital for Children, Foster's Almshouses Chapel, Colston Street, George Muller Museum, Harvey's Wine Cellars, The Old Police Station, Jacob's Wells Road, Queen Elizabeth's Hospital, Redland Chapel and The Wesley House in Charles Street.

Stephen Morris

Unbuilt Bristol: the city that might have been 1750-2050

Eugene Byrne

An astonishing selection of projects and proposed buildings – the good, the bad and the downright horrible – that didn't get off the drawing board. They range from Brunel's plans to site a railway terminal in Queen Square, a vast cemetery and botanical garden in St. Pauls, a proposed departmental store where the Bristol Hippodrome now stands, various Stalinistic plans to rebuild the centre of Bristol after the Second World War to a fabulous new concert hall on Harbourside, sadly killed off, a huge pyramid made from recycled wine bottles and a whole array of schemes for entertainment centres and new football grounds.

Sculpture in Bristol
Douglas Merritt

Bristol has an astonishing wealth of public art, figurative and abstract, enlivening its streets, parks and squares, fronting the harbourside, transforming a supermarket wall.

Much, like Rysbrack's celebrated equestrian statue of William III, is nationally important and commemorates 'the great and the good', other sculptures symbolise the spirit of Bristol enterprise, while some aim simply to amuse or please aesthetically. All told, 70 sculptures to enhance a walk around the city.

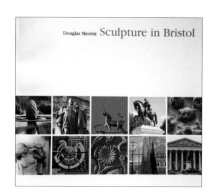

Reprinting in Autumn 2013

Bristol's 100 Best Buildings
Mike Jenner with photography by Stephen Morris

The acclaimed, entertaining and controversial selection of the city's finest buildings. Ouside London, Bristol has a far wider, and more varied, range of building types from all periods than any other city in the country. The author's sparkling commentaries are beautifully complemented by Stephen Morris's photographs.

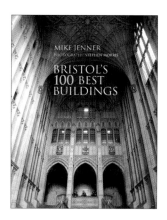

For details of all Redcliffe books see: www.redcliffepress.co.uk